YIDDISH CUISINE

My greatest joy is to experience this adventure as a family, along with my parents, brother and sisters, my husband, and my children.

They are my pillars, my anchors in the world—the most precious things I have. They give me fresh energy to carry on each day doing this hard and wonderful job.

YIDDISH CUISINE

AUTHENTIC AND DELICIOUS JEWISH RECIPES

—

FLORENCE KAHN

Photographs
Delphine Constantini

Styling
Sidonie Pain

Collection edited by
Brigitte Éveno

CONTENTS

STARTERS

MAIN DISHES

COOKING AND ITS AMAZING ABILITY TO COMMUNICATE

WELCOME TO THIS JEWISH DISTRICT OF PARIS—AND WELCOME TO MY STORE ON THE CORNER OF THE RUE DES ÉCOUFFES AND THE RUE DES ROSIERS.

This little store is more than a bakery–delicatessen. It is an ambassador for the kind of eating that is slowly disappearing. I like to think of myself as a neighborhood landmark for all those still searching for their roots. In our modern age, when the poetry of belonging is hard to come by, I hope that my store will continue to play this role for some of you.

We all need to have an anchor in life. And it's the same when it comes to roots. Because roots, well buried in the ground, are also what nourish us. Our identity and culture, Judaism, are not only passed on through religion. Food is another way in. My customers are not all religious.

I like the idea of rediscovering our roots through taste and smell—these things can remind us of the history of our ancestors, be it painful or pleasant. I took up this trade for love and I have continued through my love of it. My parents were very moved when I took over this store—in their eyes I was creating a connection between the generations, between religion and the family.

There are fewer and fewer stores run by Jewish families in this neighborhood. In my opinion, it's important to preserve a certain authenticity, a soul, to link tradition with modernity. Our store is listed as a historic building, so we can be sure that its beautiful frontage will not be destroyed.

THE RUE DES ROSIERS AND THE MARAIS

The area is full of memories for me. My great-great-grandfather, who was a rabbi, lived at number 24 rue des Rosiers and had a store on the first floor: he sold religious objects as well as clothing. When I arrived in the district in the 1980s, live chickens were still being sold in the street! For Yom Kippur, the crates of chickens would pile up and the lines would grow long in front of the Shohet (the ritual slaughterer of animals and poultry) as he carried on his work. The gutters were spattered with chickens' blood…

It was a very lively neighborhood. There was Bella who had a reply for everything and it was impossible to get out of her store without buying something; there was the fishmonger with his huge glasses who sold live carp in a tiny area of store space; there was the newspaper store where you could find hidden treasures from the world of Jewish music and literature… When the Jews arrived in this neighborhood, they bought little food stores, which meant they were sure of being able to find their own cultural products and foods.

To find four bakers in the same street isn't common! And all from the same family: cousins and brothers and sisters all linked…

Originally, the district was exclusively Ashkenazi. Then in the 1960s, North African Jews came to live and work

here, and they too bought stores. When they arrived in France, the Ashkenazi Jews had enormous ambitions for their children. In Poland, where many came from, it was impossible to own property or follow an intellectual profession. In the 1970s and 1980s, their children began to study and were able to aspire to a different sort of future. So then there was nobody to take over the family business. The stores were sold and creative studios and designers replaced the food stores. The world of fashion increased the neighborhood's popularity.

Then, in the 1980s, the area became trendy. And the gay community started to settle here. These two communities live alongside one another in perfect

harmony, respecting each other's invisible boundaries. Life is very well organized in that way. The change in habits means that everything runs smoothly, so that's good. This neighborhood has evolved but it still remains colorful today and this is what people like so much. There's a village atmosphere here, especially since the area has become part-pedestrianized. People meet outside to eat or stroll around. It's an amazing neighborhood, full of treasures. You just have to push open the doors to discover these incredible tree-lined courtyards. Here, a simple door can conceal something wonderful.

It's a never-ending spectacle. It has an extraordinary family and friendly atmosphere which, along with its cultural flavor, is unbeatable anywhere in the world. We have visitors from every country and it is easy to see why: the Jewish quarter, as in every capital, is an unmissable part of the tourist trail.

SO I INVITE YOU TO TURN THE PAGES OF THIS BOOK AND DISCOVER THE RUE DES ROSIERS—ITS SOUL, OUR STORE, AND ESPECIALLY THE WONDERS OF JEWISH GASTRONOMY.

STAR

TERS

HUMMUS

2½ cups (500 g) chickpeas, cooked

½ garlic clove

1 cup (250 g) tahini (sesame paste)

3½ tbsp olive oil

2 tsp lemon juice

1 tsp four spices

1 tsp ground paprika + a pinch for decoration

1 tsp salt

½ tsp pepper

7 tbsp very cold water

3 sprigs parsley

"" *Hummus is originally a Lebanese dish, but over time it has become a classic of Jewish cuisine, because Ashkenazi cuisine likes to be open to other food cultures.*

- Blend the chickpeas to a very fine purée.

- Peel the half clove of garlic and crush it with the blade of a knife or in a pestle and mortar.

- In a bowl, mix the tahini paste with the olive oil, lemon juice, four spices, paprika, crushed garlic, salt, and pepper. Add the cold water and leave until it has been completely absorbed by the tahini.

- Then add the chickpea purée and mix everything well with a fork.

- Decorate with chopped parsley and a pinch of ground paprika.

TARAMASALATA

9 oz (250 g) smoked cod's roe
1 egg yolk
1¼ cups (300 ml) sunflower oil
juice of ½ lemon
salt

" *Taramasalata is an adopted recipe, of Greek origin.
It is eaten in memory of the Greek Jews of Salonica.
For centuries, this town sheltered a large Jewish
community of Sephardic origin, until World War II
when most of the community was deported.*

- Carefully remove the cod's roe and discard the
  membrane surrounding it.

- Put the cod's roe in a bowl, add the egg yolk, and whisk
  with a handheld electric mixer, while very slowly
  pouring in the oil, as if you were making a mayonnaise.

- Continue to beat as you add the juice of the half-lemon.
  Add a little salt, to taste, if necessary.

TSATSIKI

1 cucumber

1 tsp salt

2 sprigs mint leaves (or the equivalent of frozen mint flakes)

2 sprigs fresh dill (or the equivalent of frozen dill flakes)

⅔ cup (150 g) smooth fromage blanc

⅔ cup (150 g) crème fraîche

pepper

- Wash the cucumber. Cut in half lengthways and remove the seeds with a large spoon.

- Grate the cucumber with a coarse grater.

- Put the grated cucumber into a sieve set over a large bowl. Sprinkle with the salt to remove the water and leave to drain.

- Wash the sprigs of mint and dill and dry them on a sheet of absorbent paper before removing the leaves and chopping them finely.

- In a large bowl, mix together the fromage blanc, crème fraîche, mint and dill leaves, and pepper to taste, using a fork. Add the grated cucumber, after removing the excess water by patting it between two sheets of absorbent paper. Mix it together and you are ready to eat.

SERVES 6
PREPARATION: 30 minutes
COOKING TIME: 1½ hours–1hour 50 minutes

EGGPLANT CAVIAR

2¼ lb (1 kg) eggplants
⅔ cup (100 g) matzah
  (unleavened bread flour)

For the mayonnaise:
5 egg yolks
½ garlic clove
1 tsp mustard
2 tsp lemon juice
2 cups (50 cl) oil
salt

" *Eggplant caviar was originally an Eastern dish that has become part of Jewish cuisine. It was so good that we couldn't resist adopting it.*

- Wash the eggplants and cut in half lengthways. Place flesh-side down on a cookie sheet lined with greaseproof paper. Cook them in the oven at 300 °F (150 °C) for 1½ to 1 hour 50 mins, depending on their size.

- Grill the skin of a third of the eggplants over a gas flame or using a blowtorch (if this is possible; otherwise place them under a broiler). Then blend all the eggplants in a mixer, including the skin.

- Prepare the mayonnaise. Peel the garlic clove, and crush it with the blade of a knife. In a large bowl, mix the egg yolks, mustard, crushed garlic, lemon juice, and salt to taste using a fork. Using a handheld electric mixer whisk the mayonnaise, gradually adding the oil. Fold in the matzah and the eggplant purée with the help of a spatula, gently mixing everything together.

- Serve chilled.

BELL PEPPER CAVIAR

2¼ lb (1 kg) red bell peppers
3 tbsp basil leaves
3 tbsp shallots
1 garlic clove
½ tsp green peppercorns
1 tbsp olive oil
½ tbsp sunflower oil
⅔ cup (100 g) matzah
  (unleavened bread flour)
1 tsp salt
pepper
ground cayenne pepper

- Pre-heat the broiler.

- Place the red bell peppers on a cookie sheet lined with greaseproof paper. Broil the peppers for about 20 minutes, turning them regularly. Remove the peppers from the broiler and immediately place in a polythene bag. Leave them to sweat in the bag for a few minutes, then rub to remove the skin, scrape out the seeds, and remove the stalk with a sharp knife.

- Wash the basil leaves, pat dry with kitchen paper, and chop finely. Peel the shallots and chop finely. Then peel the garlic clove and crush it with the blade of a knife or in a pestle and mortar. Crush the green peppercorns with a pestle.

- Slice the peppers thinly and place in a large bowl. Add the chopped basil, chopped shallots, crushed garlic clove, olive oil, sunflower oil, salt, pinch of pepper (or to taste) and the ground cayenne pepper, matzah, and crushed green pepper. Mix well.

- Serve chilled.

GREEN APPLE AND RED CABBAGE SALAD

1 red cabbage
2 green Granny Smith apples
1 lemon
4 tbsp white vinegar
4 tbsp sugar
1 tsp whole caraway seeds
4 tbsp sunflower oil
salt, pepper

- Cut the red cabbage into quarters and discard any tough outer leaves. Cut out and discard the thick white center stalks.

- Slice the cabbage into fine ribbons with a sharp knife.

- Peel and core the apples. Slice them into thin ribbons.

- Squeeze the lemon juice into a large bowl. Add the cabbage and the apple pieces. Mix well together.

- Put the mixture into a saucepan. Add the vinegar, sugar, caraway seeds, and oil, and season to taste with salt and pepper. Add a little water.

- Bring to a boil, then simmer over a low heat for 15 to 20 minutes. Serve chilled.

*In Poland, the Jews adapted kosher cuisine to suit what was locally available. Cabbage is much used in Polish cooking because it can be grown easily, keeps well, can be eaten all year round, and is very affordable.
What is more, there are hundreds of ways of preparing it: it can be eaten raw, boiled, braised, pickled ... With all these advantages, it is not surprising to find cabbage in Ashkenazi cuisine.*

JERUSALEM ARTICHOKE SALAD

8 Jerusalem artichokes
1 red onion
5 sprigs parsley, chopped
1 dash balsamic vinegar
1 tbsp Savora mustard
olive oil
paprika
salt, pepper

"
I love the Jerusalem artichoke, also known as sunchoke. It's a very cheap, overlooked vegetable that I like to cook at home. It combines the texture and generosity of the potato with the slightly bitter flavor of the artichoke. This vegetable demands a little preparation work, but what rewards it brings.

- Put the Jerusalem artichokes, unpeeled, into a pan of cold, salted water. Bring to a boil, then simmer for 15 to 20 minutes. Drain them, and now peel and cut into thick round slices with a sharp knife.

- Peel the onion and slice thinly. Wash the parsley and chop finely.

- Prepare the dressing in a large bowl: dissolve salt, to taste, in the balsamic vinegar, then add the mustard, a few drops of olive oil, pepper and paprika, to taste, and mix thoroughly.

- Put the Jerusalem artichoke slices and onion into the bowl. Pour over the dressing, mix well, and scatter over the chopped parsley.

- Serve immediately.

Served warm, this salad is utterly delicious. You can spice it up with red chili powder. It forms a marvelous accompaniment to herrings.

POTATO AND ONION PIEROGIS

2 large potatoes, mealy variety,
   such as Yukon Gold
1 red onion
2 tbsp sunflower oil
2 eggs, beaten
1 generous tbsp crème fraîche
Kreple'h pastry (see recipe p. 52)
salt, pepper

" *Or how to eat well with next to nothing. You can
eat these Polish dumplings with a little butter,
brown them with garlic in a skillet, or cook them in
the oven, covered with a dribble of tomato sauce.*

- Wash the potatoes and, without peeling them, put into a pan of cold, salted water. Bring to a boil, then simmer for about 20 minutes. Check whether they are cooked by pricking with a sharp pointed knife.

- Meanwhile, peel the red onion and cut it into small cubes of about one-third of an inch (1 cm). Brown these in the oil in a very hot skillet. Then drain, and leave aside to cool. When the potatoes are cooked, peel them before crushing with a fork. Add the beaten eggs, the crème fraiche, and the cooled onions, together with salt and pepper to taste. Adjust the seasoning if necessary, but the filling should be nice and peppery.

- Roll out the Kreple'h pastry on the worktop. Using a small, sharp knife, cut out 2½-inch (6-cm) squares. Put a little ball of the filling in the upper corner of each pastry square then fold it into a triangle. Bring together the two opposite corners of the triangle by twisting them around your finger. Press well so that the two sides are firmly sealed.

- Plunge the pierogis into a pan of boiling salted water. Let them cook for about 5 minutes. Lift them out using a slotted spoon and drain well before arranging in a serving dish. Cover with plastic stretch wrap and keep at room temperature until you are ready to eat.

SERVES 6 to 8
PREPARATION: 45 minutes
STANDING TIME: 1 hour
COOKING TIME: 30 minutes

PIROJKIS

- Prepare the dough: put all the ingredients in a mixer and knead until the dough is very smooth. Put the ball of dough in plastic wrap and place in the refrigerator for about an hour before using.

- Prepare the meat filling: peel and slice the onion. Take a large skillet, heat the oil, and brown the onion pieces until they are golden. Add the ground beef and fry until it is cooked through. Add salt and pepper, to taste, at the end of the cooking time. Put the filling to one side and leave to cool.

- Pre-heat the oven to 355 °F (180 °C).

- Remove the dough from the refrigerator. Roll it out thinly with a rolling pin. Then, using a pastry cutter, cut out circles of dough 2½ inches (6 cm) in diameter.

- Place a small ball of the cooled filling in the center of each circle of dough. Fold these in half in the shape of a small turnover, making sure that the edges are properly sealed. Line a cookie sheet with greaseproof paper and place the pirojkis on it.

- Brush the surface of each with beaten egg, to give them a glaze. Bake in the pre-heated oven for 20 minutes.

For the dough
1¾ cups (250 g) all-purpose flour
1 tbsp sugar
⅓ oz (10 g) baker's yeast; if using dried yeast follow packet instructions.
1 small egg
2½ tbsp margarine, at room temperature
¼ tsp salt
3½ tbsp cold water

For the meat filling
4½ oz (125 g) ground beef
½ onion
½ tbsp sunflower oil
salt, pepper

To finish
1 egg

Pirojkis are eaten with borscht. A spoonful of borscht, a mouthful of pirojkis … what a treat!

You can garnish these little pirojkis with different ingredients and give free rein to your imagination: A filling of spinach and goat's cheese, for example, or perhaps sauerkraut, mushrooms, or fish—or even the remains of a stew …

SPINACH TART

1 lb 2 oz (500 g) spinach
¾ cup (100 g) hazelnuts
2 eggs
7 tbsp light cream
generous ¾ cup (200 g) fromage
  blanc, drained
¼ cup (50 g) cheese, grated
olive oil
salt, pepper

For the short pastry
1¾ cups (250 g) all-purpose
  flour
salt
8½ tbsp (120 g) butter, diced
1 egg yolk
2 tsp iced water

- Prepare the short pastry: with the tips of your fingers, mix the flour and a pinch of salt with the butter and rub all the ingredients together, still using your fingertips, until you have fine crumbs. Whisk the egg yolk and iced water together, then add gradually into the flour-and-butter mix while kneading and form into a ball. Wrap and leave it to rest in a cool place, or the refrigerator, for 1 hour.

- Soften the spinach in a large pan over a low heat with a drop of olive oil. Stir well with a spatula and cook for about 10 minutes over a medium heat. Press firmly to extract as much water as possible.

- Pre-heat the oven to 355 °F (180 °C). Sprinkle the worktop with flour, then roll out the pastry thinly, to about one-eighth of an inch (3 mm). Line your tart case with it. Cover with a sheet of greaseproof paper, weighted down with ceramic or dried beans. Bake in the pre-heated oven for 20 minutes. Remove from the oven.

- Meanwhile, crush the hazelnuts with the flat blade of a knife. In a large bowl, whisk together the eggs, cream, fromage blanc, grated cheese, and salt and pepper to taste. Then add the crushed nuts, followed by the spinach. Mix gently with a fork.

- Pour the filling into the pastry case and immediately return to the oven to bake at 355 °F (180 °C) for about 30 minutes.

A very veggie dish, this tart will satisfy vegetable lovers but also all food lovers thanks to the richness of its ingredients: fromage blanc, cream, grated cheese, and hazelnuts ... mmm!

SERVES 3–4
PREPARATION: 30–40 minutes
SOAKING TO REMOVE SALT:
2–12 hours

PICKLED HERRINGS

Schmaltzherring

1 pickled Baltic herring, 11–13 oz (300–400 g)

water and milk, in sufficient quantity to cover the herring

1 onion or 1 spring onion

> *To be eaten very simply, with a thick slice of cumin bread and a few pieces of Granny Smith apple... You can then just shut your eyes and be immediately transported to the shores of the Baltic. Magic!*

- Soak the pickled herring in a mixture of half water and half milk for between 2 and 12 hours, in order to remove most of the salt, according to your taste.

- Cut off the head of the herring. With a sharp pointed knife, slit the stomach to remove the internal organs. Keep the roe or milt, which can be eaten separately.

- Next, cut the skin along the herring's back. Remove the skin by squeezing it between your thumb and the knife, moving from head to tail. Then open up the herring lengthways, squeezing the central bone between your thumb and index finger. While you are taking out the central bone, remove as many small bones as you can.

- Cut the herring in half lengthways to make 2 fillets. Clean and trim the thin skin on the sides. Rinse the fillets well under cold running water before cutting them into pieces.

- Peel the onion and cut it into thin slices (with a spring onion, it's even better).

- Place the sliced onion on top of the herring, and serve.

ZUCCHINI STRUDEL

strudel pastry (see recipe p. 128)

2 zucchini

1 garlic clove

2 tbsp flat-leaf parsley leaves

7 oz (200 g) fresh goat's milk cheese

5 tbsp smooth fromage blanc

7 tbsp whole milk

2½ tsp whole cumin seeds

2 eggs

2 tbsp flour

9 tbsp savory snack crackers, crushed

3 tbsp peanut-flavor snack crackers, crushed

½ cup (50 g) Parmesan, grated

3½ tbsp butter

salt, pepper

- Prepare the savory strudel pastry (see recipe p. 128).

- Wash the zucchini, cut off the ends, and thinly slice the zucchini lengthways using a vegetable peeler. Peel the garlic clove and crush it in a garlic press. Wash and chop the parsley leaves.

- Pre-heat the oven to 320 °F (160 °C).

- Put the zucchini ribbons briefly into a pan of boiling salted water. Drain in a sieve and rinse under cold running water to cool them down. Dry on a sheet of absorbent paper.

- In a large bowl, mix together the fresh goat's milk cheese and the fromage blanc with a fork, then thin the mixture with the milk. Add the garlic, parsley, and cumin seeds, and then mix in the whole eggs, one by one. Fold in the flour and season with salt and pepper, to taste. Add the zucchini strips and stir well.

- Mix together the cracker crumbs, the Parmesan, and the butter. Pour the cheese and zucchini mixture into the strudel pastry case. Spread the cracker crumb mix over the top.

- Bake in the pre-heated oven for 1 hour.

PUMPKIN AND HAZELNUT STRUDEL

strudel pastry (see recipe p. 128)
4¼ lb (2 kg) pumpkin
1¼ lb (600 g) hazelnuts
1 drop olive oil
salt, pepper

To finish
1 whole egg

- Prepare the savory strudel pastry (see recipe p. 128).

- Pre-heat the oven to 355 °F (180 °C).

- Peel the pumpkin, then cut it into large cubes. Put these into a big bowl with a little olive oil and season with salt and pepper, to taste. Mix well, and do not hesitate to add more pepper.

- Line a cookie sheet with greaseproof paper, place the pumpkin pieces on it and put in the pre-heated oven for about 20 minutes. Then let the pumpkin cool down to room temperature.

- Dry-toast the hazelnuts in a skillet, then chop them roughly.

- In a large bowl, mix the cooled pumpkin with the chopped hazelnuts. Spread a clean cloth on the worktop and put the ball of strudel pastry on it. Roll out the pastry with a rolling pin to about one-sixteenth of an inch (1.5 mm), then weight down each corner of the pastry so that it keeps its shape, because it is very elastic.

- Spread the pumpkin-and-nut mix over the pastry, beginning three-quarters of an inch (2 cm) from the edge. Roll up the pastry with its topping with the help of the cloth, because this pastry is very delicate and easily cracks. Carefully place the strudel on a cookie sheet lined with greaseproof paper. Brush the surface with beaten egg and bake in the pre-heated oven for 45 minutes.

PASTRAMI SANDWICH

2 slices pastrami

1 onion pletzel (see recipe p. 92)

2 tsp eggplant caviar (see recipe p. 22)

2 tsp bell pepper caviar (see recipe p. 24)

tomato slices

1 gherkin, finely sliced

" *This wonderful sandwich is famous worldwide, and nowadays is standard fare at the Rue des Rosiers. It has certainly won over the devotees of street food.*

- Cut an onion pletzel in half across its thick side.

- Spread the lower half of the pletzel with eggplant caviar then cover it with the pastrami shredded into ribbons. Add a few slivers of tomato and gherkins.

- Spread the top half with bell pepper caviar and close the sandwich. You are ready to eat.

Pastrami is beef plate or brisket that is cured with onions, garlic, and saltpeter (or potassium nitrate) for several days. The meat is turned once a day so that it "relaxes" and becomes thoroughly impregnated with the flavor of the brine. Once the meat is really ripe and mature, it is cooked in a broth and then smoked. Garlic and pepper are added, and there you have pastrami.

A PASTRAMI SANDWICH

Rue des Rosiers.

MAIN

DISHES

BORSCHT

For the beet broth
2¼ lb (1 kg) beets
white vinegar or lemon juice
salt, pepper

For the beef broth
2¼ lb (1 kg) chuck beef
1 leek
1 carrot
1 turnip
1 onion
1 garlic clove
1 celery stalk
3½ pints (2 liters) water
salt, pepper

" I prefer to make borscht in two stages: first the very concentrated beet broth and next the highly spiced beef broth. Then I combine them to give the borscht its very powerful intensity. Borscht is quite different from the generally accepted idea of it as a sad, tasteless broth. On the contrary, it is full-bodied and spicy with a very strong flavor. Just try it and you will be convinced.

- Peel the beets and cut it into small pieces. Put them in a pan containing 1¾ pints (1 liter) of cold water. Bring to the boil, add a pinch of salt and pepper, cover, and simmer for 30 minutes. Remove the lid and cook for 10 minutes longer so that the beet liquid becomes more concentrated. At the end of the cooking time, take the beet out of the broth using a slotted spoon. Then pass the broth through a fine strainer and set aside.

- Meanwhile, prepare the beef broth. Peel the leek, carrot, turnip, onion, and garlic clove. Wash the celery. Cut all the vegetables into pieces. Put the meat into a large pan containing 3½ pints (2 liters) of cold water. Bring to a boil and then turn the heat down to a simmer, all the while skimming off any froth as it rises to the surface.

- After about 15 minutes, once the broth is really clear with the froth removed, add the vegetables. Season with salt and pepper, to taste. Leave it to cook for about 1¼ hours, until the meat is tender. Remove the meat and vegetables with a slotted spoon to a serving dish and keep warm.

- Reduce the broth by simmering until you have about the same quantity of beef broth as beet broth. Pour the beef broth through a fine strainer. In a soup tureen, mix the beef broth and the beet broth in equal quantities. Adjust the seasoning if necessary with a dash of white vinegar or a few drops of lemon juice. Serve the borscht accompanied by the meat cut into pieces.

KAPUSTA BORSCHT

2¼ lb (1 kg) chuck beef
11 oz (300 g) green cabbage
1 raw beet
1 leek
1 turnip
1 celery stalk
1 tomato
¼ cup (30 g) raisins
salt

> *This is a Ukrainian specialty, but you can also find kapusta borscht in Crimea and Lithuania. The cabbage gives a hint of sharpness to the broth.*

- Put the meat into a pan containing 3 quarts (3 liters) of cold, salted water. Bring to a boil, then simmer covered with a lid for 1 hour. Skim off the froth at frequent intervals.

- Meanwhile, wash the green cabbage and cut it into fairly thick ribbons with a very sharp knife. Peel the beet, leek, and turnip, and cut into large chunks. Wash the celery and tomato. Slice the celery and cut the tomato into quarters.

- After the meat has cooked for 1 hour, add the prepared vegetables to the well-skimmed broth.

- Cook for 1 hour over a medium heat with the lid off. At the end of the cooking time, add the raisins.

- Eat this broth with beef pirojkis (see recipe p. 32).

CHICKEN AND KREPLE'H BROTH

For the broth
2¼ lb (1 kg) chicken, cut into pieces
1½ lb (700 g) carrots
7 oz (200 g) turnips
¾ lb (350 g) leeks
¾ lb (350 g) celery stalks
salt, pepper

For the kreple'h stuffing
¾ cup (150 g) ground beef
½ onion
salt, pepper

For the kreple'h pastry
generous 1 cup (150 g)
  all-purpose flour
1 small egg
salt
3½ tbsp water

This dish is so popular that I make it every week in the store. It is one of the staples of Ashkenazi food, making its appearance at every festival and whenever comfort food is needed.

- Prepare the broth: peel the carrots, turnips, and leeks. Wash and cut the celery. Put the chicken into a large pan and cover with cold water. Season with salt and pepper, then bring to a boil. Skim off the froth and add the vegetables. Simmer for about 1½ hours then remove from the heat. Pour the broth through a fine sieve.

- Prepare the kreple'h stuffing: peel the onion and slice thinly with a sharp knife. Brown the beef and onion, add salt and pepper, then leave it to cool.

- Prepare the kreple'h dough: knead all the ingredients in a food processor until the dough becomes very smooth and a little elastic. Sprinkle some flour on the worktop and roll out the dough thinly (one-sixteenth of an inch [1 to 2 mm] maximum) using a rolling pin. As the dough is elastic, keep it in place by weighting it down at each corner. Cut out 2-inch (5-cm) squares from the dough and place a little cooked meat in the center of each one. Fold into triangles, joining the two opposite corners of the triangle by twisting them around your finger. Press well to make sure the two sides are well sealed. Then lay them with the point facing upward.

- Bring a pan of salted water to the boil and put the kreple'h into the boiling water. When they rise to the surface, wait for 1 minute, then remove with a slotted spoon. Lay them in a dish covered with plastic wrap until they are cold. Reheat the broth in a saucepan and immerse the kreple'h in it for a few minutes before serving.

SPECIAL POT-AU-FEU

This pot-au-feu contains little potato dumplings. Together with the broth, it's a marriage made in heaven.

For the potato dumplings

generous 1 lb (500 g) large potatoes, mealy variety, such as Yukon Gold

generous 1 cup (150 g) all-purpose flour

1 egg yolk

coarse salt

For the pot-au-feu

3¼ lb (1.5 kg) beef (chuck, rib, shin, etc.)

1 beef bone, preferably the knuckle

2¼ lb (1 kg) carrots

11 oz (300 g) turnips

generous 1 lb (500 g) leeks

generous 1 lb (500 g) celery stalks

1 bouquet garni

salt, pepper

- Prepare the potato dumplings by peeling and dicing the potatoes. Immerse them in a pan of boiling salted water for about 20 minutes. As soon as they are cooked, drain and mash to a fine purée using a potato-masher and then fold in the flour straight away. Add the egg yolk.

- Knead the batter very quickly into a ball—it's very important that the purée stays hot during this operation. Then immediately cut the ball into slices and shape these into rolls of about half an inch (1.5 cm) in diameter. Cut the rolls into little sections measuring about one-third of an inch (1 cm). Immerse the little dumplings in a pan of boiling salted water. As soon as they rise to the surface, they are cooked. Remove them with a slotted spoon, and put them in a glass dish covered with plastic stretch wrap.

- Prepare the pot-au-feu: peel the carrots, turnips, and leeks; wash the celery stalks, then cut all into large chunks. Cut the meat into pieces. Put the meat in a pan and cover it with cold water. Add the beef bone and the bouquet garni, together with salt and pepper. Bring to a boil. Skim off any froth, then add the vegetables. Let it all simmer for about 2 hours.

- Remove the pan from the heat and strain the broth. Arrange the meat in the serving dish, with some broth poured over it. Add the little potato dumplings to warm through, then serve immediately.

GHERKIN SOUP

6 large sweet and sour gherkins
  (about a generous 1 lb [500 g])
1 leek
1 turnip
1 potato
1 carrot
1 celery stalk
1 quart (1 liter) chicken stock
1 bouquet garni
2 tbsp crème fraîche
salt, pepper

" *Gherkin soup is an amazing, highly unusual Polish recipe, but it is absolutely delicious. In summer it can be eaten chilled, served in small round glasses.*

- Grate the gherkins with a coarse grater so that they produce a thick purée.

- Peel and dice the first 4 vegetables; wash and slice the celery.

- Pour the chicken stock into a large saucepan and bring to a boil. Then add the diced vegetables and the bouquet garni. Simmer them in the chicken stock for about 40 minutes.

- Remove the pan from the heat, and add the grated gherkins, crème fraîche, and salt and pepper to taste. Mix well, and you are ready to eat.

SERVES 4
PREPARATION: 10 minutes
COOKING TIME: 15 minutes

KNEIDLERS

generous 2 cups (300 g) matzah
  (unleavened bread flour)
4 eggs
sparkling water, very cold
1 quart (1 liter) water or chicken
  stock
oil
salt, pepper

- Break the eggs into a bowl and whisk them with a fork. Gradually add the matzah, together with a little sparkling water, whisking continuously.

- Heat 1 quart of water to which you have added salt and pepper, or preferably chicken stock.

- Grease your hands with a little oil, take a small quantity of dough in your palms and shape it into little balls about the size of a walnut. Then put them into the boiling water or stock.

- When the little balls rise to the surface, wait for 3 minutes, then drain them. Arrange in a serving dish and cover immediately with plastic stretch wrap.

*Kneidlers can be eaten
with the chicken stock or
accompanied by a meat
sauce.*

SANDRINE MOSS-PISSARO'S KNEIDLERS

2¼ lbs (1 kg) onions
3 tbsp sunflower oil
½ bunch parsley
1 pinch ground cumin
½ tsp paprika
½ tsp ground ginger
pinch of four spices
1 tbsp brown sugar
2 sachets ground "Telma Kneidl"
1 quart (1 liter) chicken broth

" *Well, even I was taken in by Sandrine's kneidlers, which are a cross between the Ashkenazi and the Sephardic worlds ... After all, why not bring these traditional recipes up to date and give them contemporary appeal? Sandrine dared to do this and she was right; her recipe is delicious.*

- Peel and slice the onions. Brown them in a skillet with 1 tablespoon of oil, until they are golden. Cut the onion slices into small pieces with a pair of scissors.

- Wash and chop the parsley. Add it to the skillet with the onions, ground cumin, paprika, ground ginger, a pinch of four spices, and the brown sugar. Combine it all together with the ground "Telma Kneidl" mix.

- Grease your hands with a little oil, take a small quantity of the mix in your hands and form it into little balls the size of a walnut.

- Heat the chicken broth in a large saucepan. Put the little balls into the simmering chicken broth and cook for 15 to 20 minutes.

- Drain the balls with a slotted spoon, and put them in a glass dish covered with plastic stretch wrap. Put the broth to one side.

- When you are ready to serve, reheat the kneidlers in the chicken broth.

HERRING IN A FUR COAT

4 firm-fleshed potatoes
2 large beets, cooked
2 large carrots
4 eggs
6 herring fillets
1 onion
1 small can peas
2 large gherkins
1 bunch parsley
1 jar mayonnaise
salt, pepper

" *This dish is Russian in origin, and is served for family festivities, as a starter or a main dish. It looks very spectacular as it is often presented in the form of a very large dome, with a striking mixture of colors.*

- Wash the potatoes and, without peeling them, put them in a saucepan of cold salted water. Bring to a boil. Let them simmer for about 20 minutes, then check whether they are cooked by piercing with a small pointed knife. Put them on one side and leave them to cool.

- Peel the cooked beets. Cut half of a beet into thin slices using a small pointed knife. Then grate the rest of the beets. Peel the carrots and cook them in a saucepan of boiling salted water. They should remain firm. Grate them coarsely, using a grater with large holes. Place the eggs in a saucepan of cold water and, once the water has boiled, cook them for about 10 minutes. Put them in cold water to cool before shelling and grating them. Cut the herring fillets into fine ribbons using a small pointed knife. Peel the onion and slice thinly. Drain the peas in a sieve and rinse under cold running water. Cut the potatoes and gherkins into thin slices. Wash and chop the parsley.

- Arrange the ingredients in the following order, in a tall glass dish, in a circle with greaseproof paper on top, or in small round glasses. Spread a thin layer of potatoes over the bottom. Cover these with a thin layer of mayonnaise. Add a layer of herrings, half the sliced onion, a thin layer of mayonnaise, a layer of grated beetroot, a thin layer of mayonnaise, a layer of grated carrots, a thin layer of mayonnaise, all the peas, a thin layer of mayonnaise, a layer of herrings, the rest of the onion slices, a thin layer of mayonnaise, a thin layer of potatoes, a thin layer of mayonnaise, the gherkin slices, the beetroot slices, and a thin layer of mayonnaise. Decorate with the grated hard-boiled eggs and the finely chopped parsley.

HALUSKAHN

3½ oz (100 g) smoked goose breast
1 oz (25 g) onion
generous 1 lb (450 g) sauerkraut
1½ lb (650 g) potato dumplings (see recipe p. 54)
2½ tbsp goose fat
3½ tbsp dry white wine
1 tsp ground cumin
1 drop sunflower oil
salt, pepper

" *It was during a visit to Prague that I discovered Halusky, a traditional Slovak dish. I adapted it to the Jewish tradition by replacing the pork with goose breast, which is much tastier.*

- Pre-heat the oven to 355 °F (180 °C)

- Finely dice the goose breast and brown the pieces in a skillet over a medium heat. Remove from the skillet and set aside.

- Peel the onion and cut into thin slices. Brown in the skillet with a trickle of oil. After cooking, cut up the onion slices with scissors.

- In a large bowl, mix the sauerkraut with the diced goose, the onion, and the little potato dumplings. Add the goose fat, white wine, and ground cumin. Mix well and season with salt and pepper, to taste. Then put it all into a large cast-iron casserole.

- Put into the pre-heated oven, cover with a lid, and leave it to simmer for 30 to 40 minutes. Serve caramelized.

MOM'S MEATBALLS

2¼ lb (1 kg) ground beef
1½ lb (700 g) onions
4 slices cumin bread
2 whole eggs, beaten
1½ cups water
½ cup sunflower oil
oil for cooking
salt, pepper

- Peel and slice the onions. Brown them in a skillet with a drop or two of oil. Then drain and leave to cool.

- Meanwhile, fill a soup plate with water, soak the bread in it, then squeeze it to remove excess water. Using a fork, mix the ground beef, soaked bread, beaten eggs, a quarter of the onions, and the sunflower oil in a large bowl, until the mixture becomes nice and smooth. Add salt and pepper, to taste.

- Heat a drop or two of oil in a skillet. Grease your hands with a little oil, then shape the batter into small meatballs in your palms. Brown them in the pan on all sides, then place them in a saucepan.

- Add the rest of the browned onions and 1½ cups of water to the saucepan. Bring to the boil, then turn down the heat and cover. Cook over a low heat for 15 to 20 minutes and you will have a very tasty sauce.

If you've taken a hard knock, try some of mom's meatballs and everything will be all right.

LEEK BALLS

2¾ lb (1.2 kg) leeks
3 tbsp oil
1 egg
⅔ cup (100 g) matzah
  (unleavened bread flour)
juice of 1 lemon
salt, pepper

- Trim off any thick green leaves from the leeks, wash thoroughly, and cut the leeks across into thin slices.

- Heat a skillet with a little oil. Add the leeks. Cook them for about 20 minutes over low heat, stirring continuously. When they are cooked through, leave them to cool.

- Put the cooled leeks into a large bowl. Add the egg, salt and pepper to taste, and then the matzah, gradually mixing it in.

- Grease your hands with a little oil, take a small quantity of the mixture in your palms and shape it into little balls about the size of your palm.

- In the skillet, heat a little oil again over a high heat. When the oil is very hot, flatten the leek balls into patties, and fry them in the oil. Let them brown for 3 to 4 minutes on each side.

- Sprinkle with lemon juice and serve immediately.

STUFFED CABBAGE

" A delicious recipe that people tend to underestimate.

1 large green cabbage
generous 1 lb (500 g) ground beef (or half beef, half chicken)
1 large onion
3½ oz (100 g) cumin bread, without crusts
1 egg
3 small tomatoes
1 small garlic clove, peeled
2 tbsp sugar
⅓ cup (40 g) raisins
3½ tbsp sunflower oil
1 cup (¼ liter) water
salt, pepper

- Pull off 12 big leaves of the cabbage and remove the thick stalks. Rinse the leaves in cold water, then immerse them for 5 minutes in a saucepan of boiling salted water. Rinse them immediately in cold water to preserve their nice green color. Cut the cabbage heart into thin slices. Plunge these quickly into a pan of boiling salted water, remove with a slotted spoon, and set to one side.

- Peel and slice the onion and brown the slices in a skillet with a little oil. Put a third of the cooked onion to one side for the tomato sauce. Soak the bread in a bowl of cold water, then squeeze it in your hands. Put the ground meat in a large bowl and add the egg, cooked onions, bread, sliced cabbage heart, and oil, and season with salt and pepper. Mix together while gradually adding the water. Then, shape it into 6 meatballs.

- Place a large cabbage leaf on the worktop, then put a second leaf on top, at right angles. Place a ball of meat in the center. Fold the cabbage leaf so that it envelops the meatball, then press down and tuck in the edges so that the meat is firmly enclosed. Prepare a further 5 stuffed cabbages in the same way.

- To prepare the tomato sauce, wash 2 tomatoes, and cut into cubes. Put in a saucepan together with the browned onions, the garlic clove, salt, and pepper, and leave to simmer, for 10 minutes. Pre-heat the oven to 355 °F (180 °C). Wash and dice the last tomato. Place the stuffed cabbage in an ovenproof casserole on greaseproof paper. Spread the cubed tomatoes over the top. Sprinkle with the sugar and scatter over the raisins. Pour in the water and spread the homemade tomato sauce over the top. Season with salt and pepper and put in the pre-heated oven for 30 minutes. Cover the dish with aluminum foil and continue cooking for another 30 to 40 minutes.

SPECIAL

FESTIVALS

At Hanukah, we eat Ponchkes (*jelly doughnuts*), Latkes (*crispy potato pancakes*), and other foods fried in oil.

MINI
PONCHKES
DE
HANOUCCAH

PASSOVER VEGETABLE MATZAGNES

" I invented this recipe last year, while searching for new ways with festival cooking. I was inspired by a teatime snack served at Passover—a napoleon made of matzoth and chocolate—to make a version of lasagna, which I have called "matzagne." It's easy to make and you can vary it in all sorts of ways, giving free rein to your imagination.

For a 10-inch (25-cm) square baking pan

1 lb (450 g) prepared mixed vegetables (peas, diced sauté potatoes, diced zucchini, diced eggplant, etc.)

2 tbsp olive oil

1 onion

generous ¾ cup (200 g) heavy cream

4 whole eggs + 2 egg whites

3½ oz (100 g) Emmental, grated

matzo squares, according to the size of the pan

2 tsp salt

2 tsp pepper

- Brown all the vegetables in turn in a skillet with a little olive oil.

- Peel the onion, slice thinly, and brown in a little olive oil until it takes on a nice color. Then cut up the onion slices with a pair of scissors. Drain all the vegetables through a sieve and mix together in a large bowl. Add the cream, the 4 whole eggs, salt and pepper, and the grated cheese. Mix well.

- Pre-heat the oven to 355 °F (180 °C) and line the pan with greaseproof paper. Whisk the 2 egg whites with a fork, then pour them into a soup plate. Dip a matzo sheet into the egg white and then place it in the baking pan.

- Spread a thick layer of vegetables over the matzo square, then cover with another sheet of matzo dipped in egg white. Continue in this way until you have used up all the vegetables. Then cover it all with a final sheet of matzo without dipping it in the egg white. Cover the dish with aluminum foil.

- Cook in the pre-heated oven for 30 minutes. Remove the foil and continue cooking for a further 20 minutes.

PASSOVER SPINACH MATZAGNES

For a 10-inch (25-cm) square
  baking pan

generous 1 lb (500 g) spinach

generous ¾ cup (200 g) heavy
  cream

4 whole eggs + 2 egg whites

3½ oz (100 g) Emmental, grated

matzo squares, according to the
  size of the pan

2 tsp salt

2 tsp pepper

- Steam the spinach for 10 minutes.

- In a large bowl, mix the spinach with the cream, the whole eggs, salt and pepper, and the grated cheese. Whisk the 2 egg whites with a fork and pour into a soup plate.

- Pre-heat the oven to 355 °F (180 °C) and line the baking pan with greaseproof paper.

- Dip a matzo square in the beaten egg white and lay it in the baking pan. Spread a thick layer of spinach over the top then cover with another sheet of matzo dipped in egg white. Continue in this way until you have used up all the spinach. Cover with a final matzo square without dipping it in the egg white. Then cover the dish with aluminum foil.

- Cook in the pre-heated oven for 30 minutes. Remove the foil and continue cooking for another 20 minutes.

You can also add crumbled goat's cheese or feta cheese to the spinach.

HAMANTASCHEN

For the dough
1 cup (225 g) margarine or
   butter, at room temperature
1 cup + 2 tbsp (250 g) sugar
3 eggs
vanilla extract
generous 4 cups (600 g) flour
2½ tsp baking powder
salt

For the filling
3½ oz (100 g) prunes, pitted
3½ oz (100 g) dates, pitted
3½ oz (100 g) dried figs
7 tbsp (40 g) walnuts
6 tbsp honey

- In a large bowl, beat the softened margarine with the sugar for 3 minutes. Add the eggs one by one while continuing to beat. Add drops of vanilla extract to taste and a pinch of salt, then mix again.

- Gradually add the flour and baking powder and beat the batter well to get rid of any lumps. Wrap the ball of dough in plastic wrap and put it in a cool place for at least 30 minutes.

- Pre-heat the oven to 320 °F (160 °C) and line a cookie sheet with greaseproof paper. Using a rolling pin, roll out the dough on a floured worktop, very thinly (about one-eighth of an inch/3 mm). With a pastry cutter, or a little inverted bowl, cut out circles of dough about 3 inches (8 cm) in diameter. Lay these on the lined cookie sheet and put in a cool place.

- Prepare the filling. Put the prunes, dates, figs, walnuts, and honey in a food processor bowl and pulse briefly to achieve a coarse filling.

- Put a large blob of the filling in the center of each circle of dough. Make little open turnovers by bringing the edges of the pastry circles toward the inside. Bake in the pre-heated oven for 30 minutes.

For the festival of Purim, children usually put on a disguise. Hamantaschen, little cakes representing the ears of Haman (who plotted to destroy all the Jews of ancient Persia in a single day) have pride of place.

B R E

A D

EN

c Fre...
septe...
rechon...
ans l'enc...
parallèle
uisines de l...
hoix de cette g...
'est la gare (450 000 voyageurs jour)
qui dessert la Normandie natale d'Eric
Frechon.

BAGELS

For the dough
7 cups (1 kg) flour
½ cup (100 g) sugar
1 tbsp salt
7 tbsp (100 ml) sunflower oil
2 whole eggs
2½ tbsp water
1½ oz (40 g) baker's yeast
(for dried yeast, follow maker's
instructions)

*There's nothing like our real homemade bagels.
Once you have tasted one, you are spoilt forever.
It's an essential item in our store, and we make
it in several versions: with poppy seeds, sesame,
onions, caraway ...*

To finish
2 whole eggs
Choice of seeds or herbs: poppy,
sesame, caraway, sage, onion,
rosemary, etc.

- Pre-heat the oven to 375 °F (190 °C) and line a cookie sheet with greaseproof paper.

- In a food processor, mix all the dough ingredients, except the yeast, for 5 minutes, with the beater on the first speed setting. After 3 minutes, add the crumbled yeast, then increase the speed to the second setting for 7 minutes.

- Divide the ball of dough into pieces of equal size, about 2½ oz (70 g) each.

- Roll each piece of dough into a sausage shape about 10 inches (25 cm) long.

- Twist the dough shapes together in twos and form a circle.

- Once all the bagels are made, brush them with the whole beaten eggs and turn them over onto a layer of your chosen seeds or herbs so that they become coated.

- Place the bagels on the lined cookie sheet and bake in the pre-heated oven for 22 minutes.

BLINIS

3 eggs
3½ cups (500 g) flour
½ cup (70 g) powdered milk
2 tsp salt
2 tbsp sugar
1 oz (25 g) baker's yeast (for dried yeast, follow maker's instructions)
2 tbsp sunflower oil
about 3 cups tepid water
oil or butter for greasing

" *Traditionally, these blinis are eaten with sour cream and smoked salmon, or taramasalata and salmon—or quite simply sprinkled with sugar to satisfy those with a sweet tooth.*

- Separate the whites and yolks of the eggs. Put the flour, powdered milk, salt, sugar, egg yolks, oil, and yeast into the bowl of the food processor.

- Gradually add the tepid water until the batter has the texture of a pancake batter.

- Using an electric whisk, beat the egg whites until they form stiff peaks. Gently fold them into the batter with a spatula.

- Leave the batter to rise for a few minutes. Then warm some lightly greased little blini pans.

- Pour a ladleful of the batter into the pan until it covers the whole surface equally.

- The yeast will make little bubbles form on the surface. When they open without closing over again, it is time to turn the blini and cook it on the other side.

MAKES 10 pletzels
PREPARATION: 30 minutes
STANDING TIME: 2 hours
COOKING TIME: 25 minutes

ONION PLETZEL

Bagel dough (see recipe p. 88)
6¾ lb (3 kg) onions
¾–1 cup (100 g) poppy seeds
flour for the cookie sheet
oil for the cookie sheet

" *In English, the Jewish quarter is called "the Pletzel."*

- Prepare the bagel dough.

- Divide it into 10 balls of equal size. With a rolling pin, roll out each ball of dough so that it is flat and round.

- Leave the dough to rise for 2 hours at room temperature.

- Pre-heat the oven to 375 °F (190 °C) and grease and flour a cookie sheet.

- Peel the onions and cut them into cubes. In a large bowl, mix the onions with the poppy seeds. Spread the mix over the balls of dough and press with the palm of your hand to make it stick to the dough.

- Slightly flatten the dough balls with a rolling pin and place on the prepared cookie sheet.

- Bake in the pre-heated oven for 20 to 25 minutes.

SWEET

THINGS

MINI CHOCOLATE KI'HELE'H

3½ cups (500 g) flour
1½ tsp baking powder
1½ tsp salt
vanilla extract, to taste
¾ lb (350 g) mini chocolate chips
1½ cups (350 g) soft butter
3 eggs

" *These little cakes are eaten on Shabbat.*

- Pre-heat the oven to 350 °F (175 °C) and line a cookie sheet with greaseproof paper.

- In a large bowl, mix all the ingredients together with a spoon, except for the chocolate chips, until the batter is nice and smooth.

- Add the chocolate chips, mixing them in gently so that you do not crush them.

- Put the batter in a piping bag (without the nozzle) and pipe little heaps of the batter onto the prepared cookie sheet.

- Bake in the pre-heated oven for 9 minutes.

MAKES 30 macaroons
PREPARATION: 30 minutes a
week in advance and 30 minutes on
the day of cooking
COOKING TIME: 10–12 minutes

ALMOND MACAROONS

generous 1 lb (500 g) blanched
  almonds
2 cups (450 g) sugar
1¾ oz (50 g) untreated lemon
  (preferably organic)
3 egg whites

These traditional macaroons are made with blanched almonds, pure and white. You have to prepare the almond paste in advance—otherwise it oozes oil. But this also allows time for the almond to release all its flavors.

- Prepare the almond paste at least 1 week before making the recipe. Finely crush the almonds in a mortar and pestle. Then liquidize the whole lemon, including the skin.

- In a large bowl, mix the almonds with the sugar and liquidized lemon. Then gradually mix in 2 egg whites. Stir well, then leave this almond paste to stand in a cool place for at least 1 week.

- On the day you plan to cook, pre-heat the oven to 375 °F (190 °) and line a cookie sheet with greaseproof paper.

- Take a small quantity of the almond paste and add a very tiny bit of egg white to make it just a little softer. However, the paste should remain quite firm. Put the almond paste in a piping bag with a notched, star-shaped nozzle, size 6 or 8.

- Pipe the macaroons onto the lined cookie sheet, continuing until all the almond paste is used up.

- Bake the macaroons in the pre-heated oven for 10 to 12 minutes.

You can decorate these macaroons with glacé cherries.

MAKES 6–8 croissants
PREPARATION: 30 minutes a week in advance and 30 minutes on the day of cooking
COOKING TIME: 10–12 minutes

ALMOND CROISSANTS

" These croissants are unbelievably crisp. Some of my customers are completely addicted to them.

For the almond paste
generous 1 lb (500 g) blanched almonds
2 cups (450 g) sugar
1¾ oz (50 g) untreated lemon (preferably organic)
3 egg whites

To finish
1½ cups (200 g) slivered almonds
3–4 glacé cherries

- Prepare the almond paste at least 1 week before making the recipe. Finely crush the almonds with a pestle and mortar. Then liquidize the whole lemon, including the skin.

- In a large bowl, mix the almonds with the sugar and liquidized lemon using a fork. Then gradually mix in 2 egg whites. Stir it well, then leave this almond paste to stand in a cool place for at least 1 week.

- On the day you plan to cook, pre-heat the oven to 375 °F (190 °C) and line a cookie sheet with greaseproof paper.

- Take a small quantity of the almond paste and add a very tiny bit of egg white to make it just a little softer. However, the paste should remain quite firm. Make this almond paste into a sausage shape, then roll it over a layer of slivered almonds. Make sure it is covered on all sides because this is what gives it its irresistible crunchiness. Then bend the roll of almond paste to form a horse-shoe shape. Put half a glacé cherry in the center.

- Continue in the same way with the rest of the almond paste until you have used it all up. Arrange the croissants on the prepared cookie sheet.

- Bake in the pre-heated oven at (190 °C) for 10 to 12 minutes.

MAKES 6–8 croissants
PREPARATION: 30 minutes a week in advance and 30 minutes on the day of cooking
COOKING TIME: 10–12 minutes

PISTACHIO CROISSANTS

generous 1 lb (500 g) best-quality, whole peeled pistachios
2 cups (450 g) sugar
1¾ oz (50 g) untreated lemon (preferably organic)
3 egg whites

To finish
generous 1⅓ cups pistachios

These are a luxury version of almond croissants.

- Prepare the pistachio paste at least 1 week before making the recipe. Crush the pistachios with a pestle and mortar. Then liquidize the whole lemon, including the skin.

- In a large bowl, mix the pistachios with the sugar and liquidized lemon. Then gradually mix in 2 egg whites. Stir well, then leave this pistachio paste to stand in a cool place for at least 1 week.

- On the day you plan to cook, pre-heat the oven to 375 °F (190 °C) and line a cookie sheet with greaseproof paper.

- Take a small quantity of the pistachio paste and add a very tiny bit of egg white to make it just a little softer. However, the paste should remain quite firm. Make this pistachio paste into a sausage shapes, then roll it over a layer of pistachio nuts that you have previously crushed with the help of a knife. Make sure it is covered on all sides because this is what gives it its irresistible crunchiness … Then bend the roll of pistachio paste to form a horseshoe shape. Put half a glacé cherry in the center.

- Continue in the same way with the rest of the pistachio paste until you have used it all up. Arrange the croissants on the prepared cookie sheet.

- Bake in the pre-heated oven for 10 to 12 minutes.

MAZELNUTS

3½ cups (500 g) flour
scant 4 cups (800 g) sugar
generous 3 cups (700 g) soft
  butter or margarine
generous 1 lb (500 g) hazelnuts

"Mazelnuts" is a contraction of "mazel," meaning luck, and "hazelnuts." A little like Chinese good-fortune cookies, these biscuits come with a happy message.

- Heat the broiler.

- Prepare the dough by mixing the flour, sugar, and butter together well.

- Spread the hazelnuts out on a cookie sheet and brown them under the broiler. Let them cool before mixing into the dough.

- Pre-heat the oven to 355 °F (180 °C) and line a cookie sheet with greaseproof paper.

- Roll out the dough with a rolling pin. Cut out small circles of dough with a pastry cutter and place on the prepared cookie sheet.

- Bake in the pre-heated oven for 10 minutes.

SERVES 12
PREPARATION: 30 minutes
COOKING TIME: 1 hour

PISTACHIO CHEESECAKE

" *They go wild over my cheesecake. Just like the almond croissants, my cheesecakes have their devotees. It has to be said they are yummy.*

For a loose-based baking pan
  8 inches (20 cm) square,
  2–2½ inches (5–6 cm) deep

For the fromage blanc batter
4 cups (1 kg) fromage blanc
3 eggs
½ cup (120 g) sugar
salt
vanilla extract
¾ cup (90 g) flour or potato
  starch

For the pistachio batter
11 cups (1 kg) ground pistachios
4 cups (900 g) butter, softened
10 eggs
3 cups + 2 tbsp (800 g) sugar
⅔ cup (100 g) potato flour
generous 1⅓ cups (200 g)
  pistachios, shelled and roasted
  under the grill
oil for greasing the dish

- Pre-heat the oven to 320 °F (160 °C). Oil the baking pan.

- Prepare the fromage blanc batter: in a large bowl, beat the fromage blanc with the eggs. Mix in the sugar, a pinch of salt, and drops of vanilla extract to taste. Sift in the flour and gently mix together.

- Prepare the pistachio batter. Cut the softened butter into small pieces. In a large bowl, whisk the eggs and sugar together until you obtain a paler batter. Gradually add the soft butter while continuing to whisk. Then add the ground pistachios and potato flour. Mix it all well to avoid any lumps.

- Pour the pistachio batter into the prepared baking pan. Cover with the fromage blanc batter. Sprinkle the roasted pistachios over the top.

- Bake in the pre-heated oven for 1 hour. Leave to cool before turning it out.

MORELLO CHERRY CHEESECAKE

For a loose-based baking pan
8 inches (20 cm) square,
2–2½ inches (5–6 cm) deep

7 oz (200 g) morello cherries

For the fromage blanc batter
4 cups (1 kg) fromage blanc
3 eggs
½ cup (120 g) sugar
salt
vanilla extract
scant ⅔ cup (90 g) flour or
   potato flour

- Pre-heat the oven to 320 °F (160 °C).

- Prepare the fromage blanc batter: in a large bowl, beat the fromage blanc with the eggs. Add the sugar, a pinch of salt, drops of vanilla extract to taste, and mix. Sift in the flour and gently mix together.

- Pour the fromage blanc batter into the baking pan, filling it up to a third of an inch (1 cm) from the rim.

- Scatter the morello cherries over the surface.

- Bake in the pre-heated oven for about 1 hour.

- Leave to cool before turning it out.

If you want to keep it for several days, store at room temperature.

BILBERRY CHEESECAKE

For a loose-based baking pan
   8 inches (20 cm) square,
   2–2½ inches (5–6 cm) deep

7 oz (200 g) bilberries

For the fromage blanc batter
4 cups (1 kg) fromage blanc
3 eggs
½ cup (120 g) sugar
salt
vanilla extract
scant ⅔ cup (90 g) flour or
   potato flour

- Pre-heat the oven to 320 °F (160 °C).

- Prepare the fromage blanc batter: in a large bowl, beat the fromage blanc with the eggs. Add the sugar, a pinch of salt, drops of vanilla extract to taste, and mix. Sift in the flour and gently mix together.

- Pour the fromage blanc batter into the baking pan, filling it up to a third of an inch (1 cm) from the rim.

- Scatter the bilberries over the surface.

- Bake in the pre-heated oven for about 1 hour.

- Leave to cool before turning it out.

RASPBERRY CHEESECAKE

For a loose-based baking pan
  8 inches (20 cm) square,
  2–2½ inches (5–6 cm) deep

7 oz (200 g) raspberries

For the fromage blanc batter
4 cups (1 kg) fromage blanc
3 eggs
½ cup (120 g) sugar
salt
vanilla extract
scant ⅔ cup (90 g) flour or
  potato flour

- Pre-heat the oven to 320 °F (160 °C).

- Prepare the fromage blanc batter. In a large bowl, beat the fromage blanc with the eggs. Add the sugar, a pinch of salt, drops of vanilla extract to taste, and mix. Sift in the flour and gently mix together.

- Pour the fromage blanc batter into the baking pan, filling it up to a third of an inch (1 cm) from the rim.

- Scatter the raspberries over the surface.

- Bake in the pre-heated oven for about 1 hour.

- Leave to cool before turning it out.

SERVES 12
PREPARATION: 30 minutes
COOKING TIME: 1 hour

POPPY SEED CHEESECAKE

For a loose-based baking pan
8 inches (20 cm) square,
2–2½ inches (5–6 cm) deep

1 fromage blanc batter (see recipe p. 106)

For the filling
scant 4 cups (500 g) poppy seeds
¼ yellow untreated lemon (preferably organic)
2 cups (450 g) sugar
11 oz (300 g) apricot halves in syrup
11 oz (300 g) apricot jam
cinnamon
vanilla extract
½ cup (70 g) raisins

This filling is ideal for the poppy seed cheesecake recipe but it is also useful as a garnish for all sorts of cakes: jelly rolls, sponges, strudels, tartlets, and even hamantaschen for the festival of Purim.

- Prepare the filling: crush the poppy seeds in a grinder. Liquidize the lemon, including the skin.

- In a food processor, mix the sugar, drained apricot halves, pinch of cinnamon, drops of vanilla extract to taste, and the liquidized lemon.

- Mix again if the sugar has not melted. The batter should have a liquid consistency. Add the poppy seeds, followed by the raisins, and mix gently with a spoon.

- Leave the batter to stand in the refrigerator for at least 1 night.

- On the day you plan to cook, pre-heat the oven to 320 °F (160 °C).

- Spread the poppy seed filling over the bottom of the baking pan. Very gently, pour the fromage blanc batter on top until it is about a third of an inch (1 cm) from the rim.

- Bake in the pre-heated oven for about 1 hour. Leave it to cool before turning out.

SERVES 8
PREPARATION: 1 hour
STANDING TIME: At least 1 hour
COOKING TIME: About 1 hour
10 minutes

APRICOT, ALMOND, AND PISTACHIO STRUDEL

" *A dessert to awaken the taste buds. But be careful not to overcook the apricots.*

Strudel pastry (see recipe p. 128)

For the filling
1 apple, such as Granny Smith
5½ oz (150 g) apricots in syrup
¼ cup (30 g) slivered almonds
2 tbsp whole pistachios, shelled
4½ tbsp sugar
⅓ cup (50 g) brioche crumbs

To finish
1 whole egg

- Prepare the pastry and keep it in the refrigerator. Then prepare the filling. Peel and dice the apple. Carefully drain the apricots through a sieve. Spread the slivered almonds out on a cookie sheet and brown them under the broiler. Put a few of the broiled almonds on one side to decorate. Spread the pistachios over the cookie sheet and brown them under the broiler. Then crush the pistachios with the flat of a knife. Reserve a few crushed pistachios for decorating.

- In a large bowl, mix the apricots with the sugar and brioche crumbs. Gently mix in the slivered almonds and crushed pistachios.

- Pre-heat the oven to 355 °F (180 °C) and line a cookie sheet with greaseproof paper. Take the pastry from the refrigerator and roll it out as indicated in the basic recipe (see p. 128). Starting three-quarters of an inch (2 cm) from the edge, spread the fruit mix over the pastry. Roll up the pastry with its filling, using the cloth to help you as this pastry is very delicate and cracks easily. Carefully place the strudel on the prepared cookie sheet.

- Brush the surface of the strudel with beaten egg. Then scatter slivered almonds and crushed pistachios over the surface.

- Bake in the pre-heated oven for 45 minutes.

RED BERRY STRUDEL

Strudel pastry (see recipe p. 128)

For the filling
1 apple, such as Granny Smith
generous ¾ cup (100 g) morello
  cherries
½ cup (50 g) bilberries
½ cup (50 g) raspberries
generous ½ cup (50 g) brioche
  crumbs
4½ tbsp sugar
¾ oz (20 g) untreated lemon

To finish
1 whole egg

- Pre-heat the oven to 355 °F (180 °C) and line a cookie sheet with greaseproof paper.

- Prepare the pastry and keep it in the refrigerator.

- Prepare the filling: rinse the fruit, peel and dice the apple, pit the morello cherries, liquidize the pulp and skin of the lemon. In a large bowl, gently mix the fruits with the brioche crumbs and sugar using a fork.

- Remove the pastry from the refrigerator, and roll it out as indicated in the basic recipe (see p. 128). Starting three-quarters of an inch (2 cm) from the edge, spread the fruit mix over the pastry. Roll up the pastry with its filling, using the cloth to help you as this pastry is very delicate and cracks easily. Carefully place the strudel on the prepared cookie sheet.

- Brush the surface of the strudel with beaten egg.

- Bake in the pre-heated oven for 45 minutes.

WARDA'S HONEK LEKE'H

2 scant cups (400 g) superfine sugar
3 eggs
generous 1 lb (500 g) honey
2½ tsp baking powder
1 tsp bicarbonate of soda
1 tbsp white vinegar, to pour over the bicarbonate
1 cup (240 ml) oil
1 cup (240 ml) black coffee
5½ glasses flour

My friend Warda gave me her yummy honey cake recipe. She received it as a wedding present from Miry Winer, a cousin of whom she has fond memories and who now lives in a religious community at Bnei Brak in Israel. It's an honor for me to pass on this recipe today.

- Pre-heat the oven to 300 °F (150 °C). Grease a large baking pan.

- Put into the mixer bowl—scrupulously respecting this order—the sugar, eggs, honey, baking powder, bicarbonate of soda, and white vinegar.

- While continuing to mix, add the oil, black coffee, and flour.

- Pour the batter into the cake pan so that it is three-quarters full.

- Bake in the pre-heated oven for 1½ hours.

GLUTEN-FREE SHABES QUEEN WITH PISTACHIO

½ cup (60 g) pistachios
1½ oz (45 g) dark chocolate
¾ packed cup (120 g) soft dark brown sugar
⅔ cup (150 g) margarine, melted
3 eggs
⅔ cup ground hazelnuts
⅔ cup (100 g) rice flour
2 tsp baking powder
butter for the cake tin
salt

"*I created this dish to respond to the demand for gluten-free desserts. It's just as delicious with macadamia nuts broken into large pieces (sweet or salty, toasted in the oven or cold). Or why not with raisins, blueberries, or sunflower seeds?*

- Pre-heat the oven to 355 °F (180 °C) and butter a cake pan.

- Crush the pistachios with a flat blade. Grate the dark chocolate with a coarse grater.

- In a pan, melt the sugar with the margarine, whisking it continuously.

- Separate the egg whites and the yolks.

- Using an electric whisk, whisk the egg whites with a pinch of salt until they stand up in stiff peaks, then put to one side.

- In a large bowl, slowly stir the egg yolks with a spatula, then mix in the crushed pistachios, ground hazelnuts, grated chocolate, rice flour, and baking powder. Mix well. Add the beaten egg whites, folding them in gently with a spatula.

- Pour the batter into the prepared cake pan. Bake in the pre-heated oven for about 45 minutes.

VERY SIMPLE AND VERY GOOD GLUTEN-FREE SHABES QUEEN

3 eggs
4½ oz (125 g) dark chocolate
½ cup (110 g) butter or
  margarine
⅔ cup (100 g) sugar
2 level tbsp cornstarch
butter for the cake pan
1 pinch salt

- Pre-heat the oven to 355 °F (180 °C) and butter a cake pan.

- Separate the egg whites and the yolks. Cut the chocolate and butter into pieces.

- Melt the chocolate and butter in a bowl set over a saucepan of simmering water. Add the sugar and whisk until the sugar has completely melted. Fold in the cornstarch.

- Remove the bowl from the double boiler. Stir the batter well, then let it cool to room temperature. Add the egg yolks and stir well.

- Using an electric whisk, whisk the egg whites with the pinch of salt until they stand up in peaks. Add the beaten egg whites to the chocolate batter, gently folding them in with a spatula.

- Pour the batter into the prepared cake pan.

- Bake in the pre-heated oven for about 20 minutes.

APPLE CAKE

¾ lb (350 g) Gala or Golden
  Delicious apples
generous 1⅓ cups (200 g) flour
1¾ cups (200 g) confectioners'
  sugar
4 eggs
1¼ tsp baking powder
⅔ cup (160 g) margarine, at
  room temperature
butter for the cake pan(s)

- In a large bowl, mix the flour, sugar, eggs, and baking powder. Add the softened margarine last, without mixing it in too much.

- Peel the apples and cut them into small pieces. Gently add them to the batter with a spatula.

- Pre-heat the oven to 355 °F (180 °C) and butter the cake pan.

- You can make this cake either in a large size, or as a batch of small cakes. Bake in the pre-heated oven for 30 to 35 minutes for the large size or 12 to 15 minutes for the smaller ones.

You can also mix pears and apples, in equal quantities.

SWEET OR SAVORY STRUDEL PASTRY

7 cups (1 kg) flour
1¼ cups (300 ml) water
5 eggs
½ cup (120 ml) sunflower oil

Sweet strudel pastry:
¾ cup + 2 tbsp (200 g) sugar

Savory strudel pastry:
1 tsp salt

- In a food processor, mix the flour, water, eggs, and oil with the beater paddle, then add the sugar or salt, depending on how you are going to use the pastry. Increase the speed and leave it to turn—the pastry has to become warm and stick to the side of the food processor bowl.

- Put the ball of pastry in a dish covered with plastic stretch wrap and place it in the refrigerator for at least 1 hour.

- Spread a clean cloth on the worktop and put the ball of pastry on it. With a rolling pin, roll out the pastry thinly, to about one-sixteenth of an inch (1.5 mm). Stretch it to the maximum and weight it down at each corner to hold it, because it is very elastic.

- Use the pastry according to your recipe.

PREPARATION: 15 minutes
STANDING TIME: 15 minutes
COOKING TIME: 15 minutes

GLUTEN-FREE PASTRY FOR SWEET TARTS

generous 1⅓ cups (200 g) rice
  flour
1½ tbsp vegetable margarine
2½ tbsp stewed apple
⅓ cup (30 g) ground almonds
1 whole egg
2 tbsp sugar

- Pre-heat the oven to 355 °F (180 °C).

- Remove the margarine from the refrigerator and leave it to soften to room temperature.

- Mix the softened margarine with the stewed apple using a fork. Add the ground almonds, followed by the egg and sugar. Mix well.

- Then fold in the rice flour.

- Make the pastry into a ball and place it in the refrigerator for 15 minutes.

- To roll out this pastry, it is best to put it between 2 sheets of greaseproof paper before you roll it with the rolling pin.

- Bake in the oven at 355 °F (180 °C), either unfilled (weighted down with pie weights, "blind-baked") or with a filling, for 15 minutes.

FLORENCE KAHN

The store

Come and see us
24, rue des Écouffes
(at the corner of 19, rue des Rosiers),
75004 Paris

01 48 87 92 85

You can also find us at our online store:
www.florence-kahn.fr

INDEX

MEASUREMENTS

LIQUID VOLUMES

Metric system	American system	Other names
5 ml	1 teaspoon (French coffee spoon)	
15 ml	1 tablespoon (French soup spoon)	
35 ml	⅛ cup (French cup)	1 oz (or ounce)
65 ml	¼ cup or ¼ large glass	2 oz
125 ml	½ cup or ½ large glass	4 oz
250 ml	1 cup or 1 large glass	8 oz
500 ml	2 cups or 1 pint	
1 liter	4 cups or 2 pints	

DRY VOLUMES

Metric system	American system	Other names
30 g	⅛ oz	
55 g	⅛ lb	2 oz
115 g	¼ lb	4 oz
170 g	⅜ lb	6 oz
225 g	½ lb	8 oz
454 g	1 lb	16 oz

OVEN TEMPERATURE

Heat	° Celsius	Thermostat	° Fahrenheit
Very low	70 °C	Th. 2–3	150 °F
Low	100 °C	Th. 3–4	200 °F
	120 °C	Th. 4	250 °F
Medium	150 °C	Th. 5	300 °F
	180 °C	Th. 6	350 °F
Hot	200 °C	Th. 6–7	400 °F
	230 °C	Th. 7–8	450 °F

I would like to thank all those who have contributed (intentionally or not) to this book:

My parents, Raymonde and Jacques Kapota, for their unconditional love; My brother, Alain Kapota, for his constant support, confidence, and devotion in running this store and being by my side for over 25 years; My sisters and brothers-in-law, Dalith and Shimon Castiel, and Minou and Tsvi Jakubowicz, for their overwhelming confidence and wise counsel; My husband, Willy Ventura, for the love he shows me and the happinesss with which he surrounds me each day My children Laura, Dimitri and Natasha Finkelsztajn, who won me the contest for the prettiest mum in the world; My stepchildren, Joanna, David, Yaacov, Shemuel, Naomi, Ruthy and Eytan Ventura, without whom my life would not be what it is today; Michèle and Francis Bloumels for having helped me through difficult times, and believing in me more than anybody; My daily team of people who make, develop, suggest, arrange, decorate, and sell all the good things in our store: Azzedine, Marie-Noëlle, Didier, Sophie, Hassan, Aminour, Javier, Maria, Sassi, Vazi, Vesna, Koumar, Ghislaine, Allala, Daniela, and Alexia, as well as those who have worked with me over all these years; Claude Friedman, Sandrine Moss-Pissaro, and Varda Schoenbach, for their recipes, little secrets or other anecdotes; My customers, whether they are regulars or just passing through—without them this store could not continue; My sincere and wholehearted thanks to all of you (and I hope not to have forgotten anyone).

Florence Kahn

Sidonie Pain warmly thanks

Astier de Villatte, www.astierdevillatte.com
Martine Ménard ceramicist, martine-menard.fr
and Emma Challier, www.emmachallier.com
for their invaluable assistance.

Thank you

to Florence, for her generosity, her spontaneity, and of course her delicious recipes with their flavor of my forebears… a felicitous union.
To Brigitte and Marine, for their kindness and trust.
To Jean-Marc and to all my family and close friends for their unwavering support.
To my daughter Shirel, my most exquisite gift, thanks for her love of life which fills my heart and influences many of my pictures …

Delphine Constantini

Disclaimer

It is advisable not to serve dishes that contain raw eggs to very young children, pregnant women, elderly people, or to anyone weakened by serious illness. If in any doubt, consult your doctor. Be sure that all the eggs you use are as fresh as possible.

Layout and creation of the interior and cover: Patrice Renard
Photogravure: Amalthéa
Preparation of copy and corrections: Isabelle Clémenceau
Editing: Marine Schoeser
Production: Thierry Dubus

© for this English edition: h.f.ullmann publishing GmbH

Translation from French: Rosemary Rodwell in association with First Edition Translations Ltd, Cambridge, UK
Editing: Lin Thomas in association with First Edition Translations Ltd, Cambridge, UK
Typesetting: Paul Barrett Book Production in association with First Edition Translations Ltd, Cambridge, UK

Overall responsibility for production: h.f.ullmann publishing GmbH, Potsdam, Germany

Printed in India, 2016

ISBN 978-3-8480-1028-8
10 9 8 7 6 5 4 3 2 1
X IX VIII VII VI V IV III II I

www.ullmannmedien.com
info@ullmannmedien.com
facebook.com/hfullmann
twitter.com/hfullmann_int

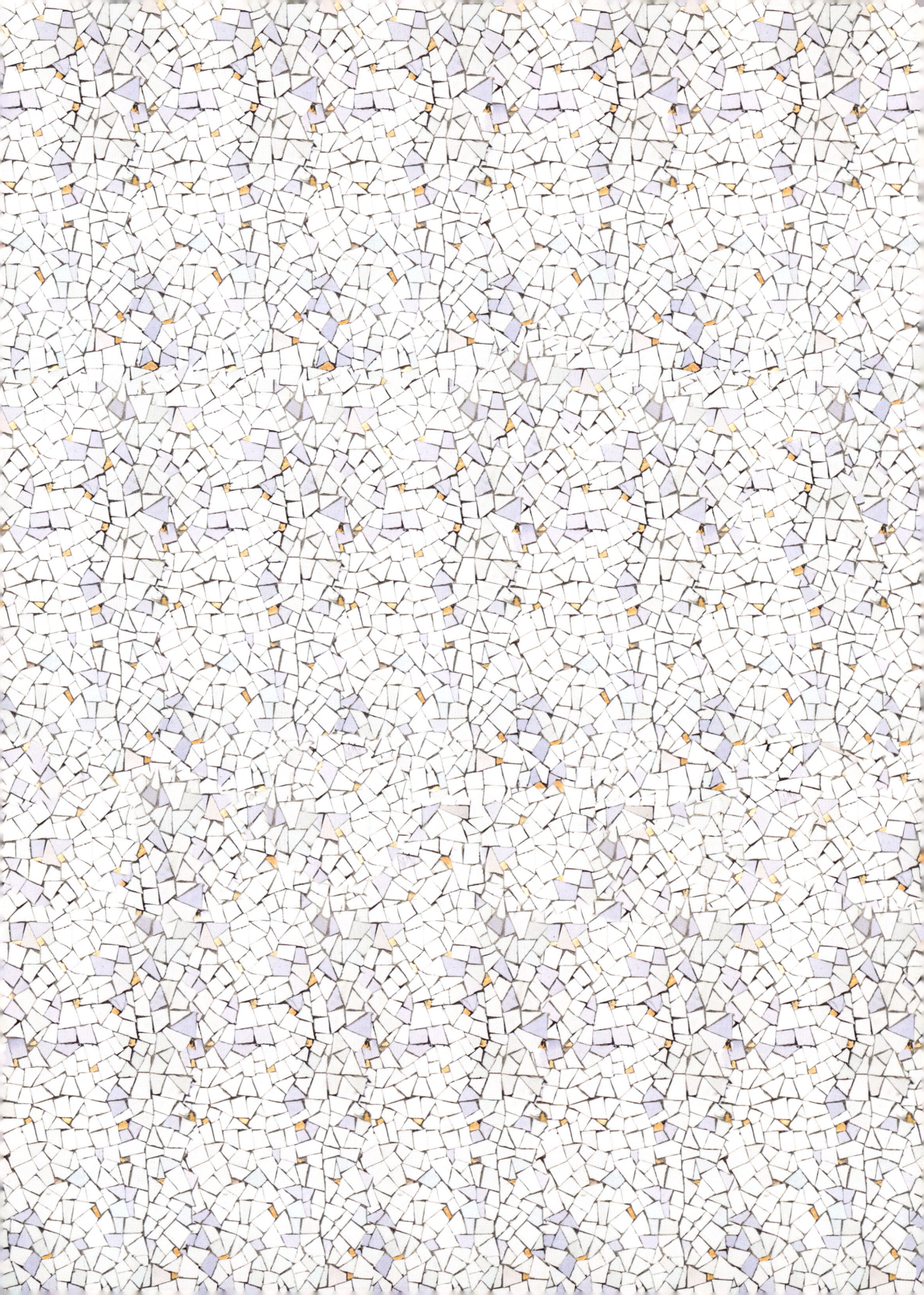